I live in Devon and I am ver
and the sea nearby, which I
rhymes. I live with Diane, my partner, and we have a cat
called B and a dog, called Charlie, which we rescued and
who never stops wagging his tail. I wrote about this in
The Tail of the Waggy Dog. A lot of my work for many
years has been with Deaf people, communicating in their
wonderful language of Sign Language which I hope
comes across in my poem, *Talking with Dancing Hands*.

The Rhythm of Rhyme

Steve Almy

The Rhythm Of Rhyme

Nightingale Books

NIGHTINGALE PAPERBACK

© Copyright 2018
Steve Almy
Illustrations by Julia Puig Banchs

A CIP catalogue record for this title is
available from the British Library.

ISBN 978 1 907552 95 3

*Nightingale Books is an imprint of
Pegasus Elliot MacKenzie Publishers Ltd.*
www.pegasuspublishers.com

First Published in 2018

**Nightingale Books
Sheraton House Castle Park
Cambridge England**

Printed & Bound in Great Britain

Dedication

This book is dedicated to my mum and dad, Bob and Pat (Bunny).

Acknowledgements

To Charlotte, my daughter, who, since she was very small, has always related to my stories and rhymes and has been a huge support in putting this book together.

THE WORD WIZARD

From the very, very young

To the very, very old,

There's a story to be sung

Or a story to be told.

So put your wizard hat on,

Catch the words that spin around

And wherever you may be,

Make sure you write them down.

SUNRISE

Who paints the pictures

With every sunrise

To make the world so beautiful

With colour in the skies?

The emerald sea that glitters

On a starry, starry night,

Red sky in the evening,

A shepherd's delight.

<u>CLOUDS</u>

What shape do they make in the sky?

A rabbit or a pig that can fly?

Of course pigs don't fly;

They haven't got wings!

It's only a cloud!

But a cloud can be anything

If you just stop and stare;

There's a whole wide world

Waiting up there!

TWO FLINT STONES

Our story begins

When we lit the first fire

With two flint stones,

A long time after the dinosaurs roamed,

Keeping them burning day and night,

And painting the walls in the glimmering light.

But now,

Though it's so easy at the flick of a switch,

Never forget,

History was made,

Back in the caves,

With those dry leaves and sticks!

FASHION

Many fashions have appeared over the years

But I don't think Stone age people really cared

What to wear, when being chased by bears,

Dressed in fur, from their toes to their ears

While hunting around with clubs and spears.

But over time came design,

Leathery, Feathery

Silly, frilly

Bright, tight, itchy, titchy

Flat caps, top hats, flairs

Beehive hair

And Dickie bow ties.

They've tried them all in every size

And then when it gets boring

and time for a change

You'll often find they're trendy again.

A TRICKLE OF RAIN

A trickle of rain is not what it seems

Because a trickle of rain can soon make a
stream;

And where , you may ask, does it go when it
flows?

Into a river that gets bigger and bigger,

Like the Nile with style that winds along

Or the Mississippi with its music and song;

And sometimes it drops down and down,

Like Niagara Falls with its crashing sounds;

And then it calms back to a gentle stream;

You see a trickle of water is not what it seems.

AIR, LIGHT, RAIN, AND SOIL

In our ready-made society

Of KFCs and Maccy Ds

Spare a thought for the potato

And how it grows

A tiny grain

Sitting there in the soil

Feeding on air, light and rain

Then, out it comes, ready to boil

Cut in bits to make the chips

Into a box made from a tree

Which came from a grain

That sat in the soil

And fed on the air and the light

And the rain

BITS AND BOBS

Someone said, "It's bits and bobs. We'll talk
about today."

And then I started thinking, what did she really
say?

And, looking for an answer, I found its history;

A bob: a shilling or twelve pence; a bit is only
three.

'Raining Cats and Dogs', no explanation can be
found;

Frogs, yes, as once they did pour down.

Stories over centuries, from the land to the
sea;

Words from France or Germany.

Latin words when the Romans came,

Different spelling but sound the same:

Nose like knows; through like threw ; poor like paw;

So, when you come across a word you've never heard before,

It might remain a mystery, just part of old folklore;

And even in the strangest places the old mix with the new;

"I need to spend a penny," is to use the ladies' loo.

THE LEGEND OF KING ARTHUR

He rides upon a stallion with a shiny jet black
coat

And lives upon a hilltop in a castle with a moat.

Here inside his castle sits a king upon his
throne.

Arthur is his name and Tintagel is his home.

Everywhere he looks, he can see for miles
around,

From the boats across the sea to his people on
the ground.

A fair and honest man, he is known across the
land

For protecting all his people, Excalibur in his
hand.

A wondrous sword with special powers, he
pulled it from the stone,

It was waiting there for many years, always his
to own.

King Arthur, many friends had he, and the
special ones were knights,

Bravely they would follow him and bravely
they would fight.

Side by side they would ride to search for the
ancient Holy Grail

O'er every hill and mountain, every road and
trail.

This legendary cup still somewhere lies buried
in the ground;

Though Arthur searched a lifetime, it was
never to be found.

From John O'Groats to Land's End his search
went on and on;

One day you might discover it shining in the
sun.

Though his castle may be crumbling from the
Cornish stormy weather,

The Legend of King Arthur will live on forever

With his faithful knights and Excalibur, the
sword in the stone,

Merlin and his potions and the magic he has shown.

<u>ACROSS THE MOOR</u>

When you go walking across the moors

You may come across some rocks called tors

Which millions of years ago or so

Would have been full of dinosaurs.

But the earth started wobbling and thrashing around,

And up they all popped as the lava rushed down.

Then suddenly it all stopped and turned to stone

and now these rocks stand alone,

tall and proud

As the children climb to their peaks and shriek out loud.

Though the seasons may change,

They stay exactly the same,

Watching the world go by

As the sun shines down or the snowballs fly.

A FIELD OF SOUNDS

Stand in a field,

Surrounded by trees,

And listen

To the sounds around;

A gentle breeze,

The rustling of leaves,

Picking up and slowing down.

Looking around,

My ears are my eyes.

A sudden movement fills the skies,

And then,

Subsiding,

The rhythm begins again.

COLLECTING POLLEN FROM THE FLOWERS

One, two, three, I'm a bee,

And someone has been here before!

But that's OK, there is plenty more

Here in flower number four.

Then, later on, when the pollen has grown,

I'll go back to number one,

Then number two, then number three,

Cos I'm a busy, busy, busy bee!

ADVENTURERS AND EXPLORERS

There have been people throughout history

Who walked the earth or sailed the seas,

Sometimes with nothing more

Than wooden sticks or wooden oars,

Guided only by the stars, no radios!

They would battle huge waves or drifting snow

To discover the places that we know:

The North Pole, the South Pole, Australia,
America,

Men like Scott or Cook, what courage it took!

So frightened, so cold; the stories we're told

Which shape the world for all boys and girls;

Adventurers and Explorers and Pioneers

Who faced their fears to find new frontiers.

THE BEAUTIFUL SEA

Slip away quietly on a cold, starry night

With the wind in your sails and the moon for a
light,

Silently crossing the deepest blue sea

And wonder tomorrow where you will be;

Maybe in France? Ooh la la!

Eating escargots or dancing cha- cha?

Or maybe in Spain where it rains on the plains?

Upon the wide ocean is never the same;

Then when the sun rises up on a warm,
cloudless sky,

The dolphins come smiling and stay by your
side,

Dipping and diving as they love to do,

And they'll chuckle away as if they're talking to
you!

So let the white horses run and the strong
winds blow

To take you safely wherever you go,

Near or far, just follow your Star!

Because wherever you may be,

You're never alone on The Beautiful Sea!

THEATRE

They drew up their wagons

And pulled out their drums;

"Roll up! Roll up! It's time, everyone,

To gather round and have some fun!"

And that is how the theatre began,

In the market places and open air spaces,

Or in a barn if it rained,

Collecting loose change,

But if no-one came, they just moved on

To search elsewhere

With their music and song;

And though the stages have gone,

The entertainment lives on

In the grandest of theatres

In New York and London.

THE INDIAN SUMMER

Sometimes in late September

Summer comes back here again,

And if it's been raining in holiday time

That can be a really big shame.

Perhaps it was okay for the Indians

When they hunted the buffalo plain,

But stuck inside on this hot day

I don't care about how it was named!

PIRATES

"Come on, me hearties, there's treasure aboard!"

Then he swung on his rope and waved his sword.
With earrings dangling from his ears

And with crusted salt on his long black beard,

He ran across the deck like a bouncing gazelle

And stood at the bow,

"All will be well," he started to say,

"If you give up the gold, we'll sail away!"

And this they did and the pirates hid it

In a place marked with an X to show exactly where,

But they sometimes forgot it was even there!

So the next time you're digging and you hear a loud 'clunk',

Go very carefully round it as it may not be junk!

You may find a box very special and old,

A chest full of diamonds and glittering gold!

CASTAWAY TOM AND THE TAILS OF THE WHALES

Castaway Tom has a very long beard,

That he's grown since last year's storm.

When near to the shore, there was a gentle breeze

And the clouds were gathering over the seas.

The gentle breeze, it grew and grew

Until a wild wind blew and blew!

Hissing spray and bubbling foam!

Then suddenly the storm was gone

And Tom was shipwrecked alone.

Each morning two parakeets went, "chirpy, cheep, cheep!"

Each night he would sleep on a bed of gold,

Which would make him rich until he was old;

And then, one day, Tom was out in the bay

Waiting for his friends, the whales, to play;

When "Whoosh! Splish, Splash, Splush!"

Their tails made a wave... and he sailed away!

WHITE HORSES

The wind is whipping across the bay

Flecks of foam, flecks of spray

Along the waves, they call White Horses.

Force four or more,

The storm clouds brewed,

And, as the wind blew, they galloped along,

Fifty thousand strong,

And then they were gone;

Just a shimmering sheen,

As if the White Horses had never been!

THE WAVE SURFER

Arms aching,

Skittering like a crab through the breaking
waves,

A final push,

To wait patiently

For lines to come across the sea,

And then with a surge

And a skip,

Standing tall,

Racing with nature

As it tumbles and falls.

LILLY AND THE CRICKETS

"Please, Mummy, can we go and cool down in the puddle by the pool?" the crickets all cried and waited wide-eyed.

"OK, just for a moment," she replied. And quick as a flash, they were in with a splash, laughing and giggling without a care in the world.

They were having so much fun they didn't see the little girl at the side, getting ready to dive, or hear Mum's calls above the noise, who then stopped and poised (like a ballet dancer, ready to leap into the air).

Suddenly, water rained down from everywhere, sweeping everything in its way and as she hurtled along she found a petal, she clung onto and stayed.

Soon it slowed to streams and blobs that glistened and glowed and with a bump, off she jumped. Shivering and quivering Mum tried to stand, when in the shape of a cup came two little hands.

They picked her up and held her as gently as they put her down and when she turned round there was Loulie Lou and Eric, her boy, and they danced and hugged with tears of joy.

Meanwhile, the little girl, whose name was Lilly knew there was one more and began to search for cricket number four. Even though it might have looked a bit silly, Lilly went down on her knees and started to turn over all of the leaves. Then, as she got tired and thirsty, she stopped for a drink when something hopped in with a 'Plop' and a 'Clink' and scooping out whatever it was over the rim, she let it dry out on top of her skin.

All floppy and soggy it started to grow, kicking out one leg then two and what do you know? It pushed itself up on its tiny front paws and there was cricket number four!

It sat very calm and still, looking ahead as they walked along, while Lilly sang her brand-new song;

"Four, then three, then two, then one,

I'm a little cricket sitting in the sun."

As she lowered her arm into the bush, Lilly watched them all skip happily away, and thought how pleased she felt helping the little cricket family today.

TALKING WITH DANCING HANDS

Though my ears don't work,

There are many ways to talk.

So, what about "Hello"?

A wave of the hand, someone knows you're there,

But a smile shows you care.

And in your eyes

You hear calls and cries;

A look says so much.

And then there's the gentle touch;

So the next time the wind blows through the trees,

Watch the dance of the dangling leaves,

Let the breeze make brushstrokes on your face,

Just like the silent world of sign,

Intricate, beautiful and full of grace.

THE WEDDING PHOTO

We held the word above our heads,

Tied up by four strings,

But someone let a letter go

And off it floated in the wind;

Then we all laughed and no one cared

It now spelt L... O... V

Because though the E fell out of love

Love didn't fall out of E

MR NOBODY

Sometimes there are certain people who can
only be mean,

Writing behind screens in a world unseen,

Throwing out words like a game of darts,

But who would run a mile if they heard a fart!

So NO, Mr Nobody, you will not take away

My freedom and liberty

And as I move on,

And your smile has gone,

Who's laughing now?

Yes, who's laughing now?

Yes, who's laughing now,

At the tricks of a clown!

SUPERHEROES

Who would you choose to be?

A Superman or Supergirl

Spinning round

Who in a flash saves the world.

And what would you wear

On the Planets and Stars out there?

A spider's web or yellow and red

A suit with boots that bounce like balls

And special gloves to climb the walls?

Shiny black or charcoal grey

Is the colour of the rocket to the Milky Way;

Past the moon with an extra zoom,

Engines reversing, flaps now down :

"Mission control, we're on the ground,

Ready for tea and dreams of the day

When the Superheroes saved the day!"

BUBBLES ON THE WATER (kitesurfing)

Holding onto bubbles,

Dancing on the sea,

Poetry in motion

In perfect harmony;

All the colours of the rainbow

Are floating in the sky,

As they skim across the ocean

And somehow try to fly.

BUBBLE AND SQUEAK (Two Sqirrels)

Silently skipping across the woodland,

With the nuts they have found,

Suddenly they sit bolt upright,

When they hear a sound,

Waiting motionless, as if holding a cup.

Tails up!

A quick look around,

And then, like acrobats elegantly climbing the trees,

Across the branches they trapeze,

And then fly, legs and arms open wide,

All summer long.

And then, they are gone;

To hide away in their drays

Sleeping till the warm weather starts and stays.

And then, one by one, out they come,

Finding their nuts and having fun

And being enjoyed by everyone.

THE SHEEP THAT GOT STUCK IN THE WIRE

I was looking over the gate of a field full of
sheep,

When I suddenly heard

A solitary bleat.

I leaned further over

Just a bit higher

And saw a young lamb that was caught in the
wire.

Not all of it;

Just its head:

Wriggling its bottom and pushing with its legs.

So I ran over quickly and held on tight

And pulled at the fence

With all of my might.

Then out she came;

Happy again;

Jumping four feet

With the happiest bleat!

THE TREE

How old are you?

How many winds have passed on through?

How many birds have played their tunes?

The nightingale, the owls, the moon

Have danced upon you day and night;

In rustling leaves the birds take flight.

How many seasons come and go?

The mist, the rain, the drifting snow.

How many skies have you seen?

How many sunsets have there been?

Glows of sunlight sinking low,

To rise again, a brand new show!

In summer's heat you grow and spread;

In winter's cold your leaves you shed;

Ocean's green and flaming red.

Birds and bees and little bugs,

Made you their home to love and hug.

A thousand worlds just passing through.

Without you trees, what would we do?

MOUNTAINS

How many years since Man first laid his hand
upon this land,

That we call home where dinosaurs once
roamed?

And then, with a roar,

The Earth rumbled and tumbled and out of the
dust,

The mountains soared!

And now, in awe, I watch

As the eagle flies down

And grabs its prey,

No place to run and then up and away.

And the snows that come and go

Melt in the sun;

Another season has begun,

Trickling and then rushing down.

In every precious drop, a wonder to be found.

What we take away, we must always put back
today

And cherish the land so the children can play.

IN THE BLINK OF AN EYE

We smiled through the windows,

So close we could touch;

And then from 'bunny hops'

We went with a rush!

Sheep and cows we could hardly see,

Rolling hills, houses and trees.

Faster and faster,

In the blink of an eye,

The world speeding up and flashing by!

Then slow, stop, stare

At the lines of cars stretching everywhere.

Where are they going?

What do the people do?

I smiled through the window,

But it wasn't you!

THE HERON

Sometimes I look at the dawn,

Crispy and misty with so much going on,

And that's when they say;

"The early bird catches the worm."

Like yesterday, at seven a.m.

A flock of seagulls came by;

"Mike, Mike, Mike," I heard them cry,

And as I watched them overhead,

I noticed a bird with spindly legs

Open wide its wings and glide

Onto the rooftop below,

Where it stopped on top

With its long thin toes

And then settled down;

It craned its neck and looked towards

The rivers, the lakes, the ponds,

And there it was,

The proud, beautiful, white heron!

WILD SWIMMING

Wild swimming is what it's called,

But it's not like crossing the Colorado or
jumping off Niagara Falls!

It's just a little river that runs through the
moors,

Down to the sea, down from the tors.

Often gentle but when the snow melts or when
the rain pours down,

The river rises and rushes around,

Slicing past the rocks, with gurgling and
spitting sounds.

But here today it's only a flutter of a breeze
that comes

To sparkle patches in the sun;

And then, while it's calm, step in

And look at your arms and notice your skin

Has changed orange to white,

A trick of the light.

Through dark treacle coloured water that laps side to side

Swim to the bank where the dragonflies fly,

Sparkling blue and purple, turning circles high and then wide,

They stop, completely still, if they sense danger nearby.

'Camouflaged green', so they can't be seen, they wait it out.

Then slowly they start popping about!

And with gentle strokes, so as not to disturb again, back you swim,

Full of the wonders of the places you've been.

MOTOR RACING

There's a new model on the Grid.

I bet it cost more than a quid!

Waiting, purring with the others down the line,

Then off

o to 60 every time!

Red Bull in front,

Mercedes just behind,

A quick pit stop,

Ten seconds on the clock,

Tyres are changed,

Then back out again,

Round the bend,

Then on the straight,

The last leg home.

He waits, overtakes

And the flag goes down!

The corks pop and the champagne is sprayed around!

The champion bows and receives his crown!

THE TITANS OF THE TENNIS COURT

We ate strawberries and cream as we sat in the crowd

And then, like lions, we roared out loud!

As the players came on for the very first serve,

When, all of a sudden, not a pin drop was heard.

Then tick tock, tick tock,

Backwards and forwards, like the sound of a clock;

Left, right, left, right, heads turn in perfect harmony;

Thirty, thirty-one, thirty- two, thirty-three.

Rally after rally;

Till finally, we're out of our seats,

Onto our feet!

As the winner falls down and kisses the grass,

The title of Champion is won at last!

PEPPER AND SALT

A sprinkle of pepper, but where is it from?
A tropical fruit dried out in the sun;

A little bit of salt, you hear it crunch,

And then a pinch and you put it on your lunch,

On mash, perhaps, with a sausage and some
sauce,

And a couple of slices of bread, of course.

Delicious!

In fact, pepper is very, very old

And among the first spices to be bought and
sold,

When it crossed the lands,

With cumin and saffron in the caravans,

Pulled by camels, plodding along the trails,

And then put onto the boats they used to sail.

So the next time you eat

And there's spice in your tea,

Remember the tastes

Have a long history!

IF I WERE THE CAPTAIN OF A TALL SHIP

If I were the captain of a Tall Ship,

Just for one day,

I'd like to find where the mermaids play;

And with the wind in my sails,

On a sea so blue,

I'd search to see if they were really true:

The mysteries of the serpents far below,

Green-eyed monsters and the places they go;

And then, of course, the stories told

Of pirates and where they hide their gold.

I wonder if Bluebeard was very, very old!

And what about all those tales

Of Moby-Dick and Jonah and the Whale?

But I'd only go on a gentle breeze,

Not holding on through mountainous seas,

And, then, safely back home from this wonderful day:

"Aye aye, Captain!" is what they'd all say!

TRAVELLING JOEY

Did you know

That a kangaroo can hop thirty feet or so

Even with a joey asleep in her pouch?

That's how far she can go

Inside a pouch on her Mother's tum

Being a travelling Joey must be so much fun.

CAT IN THE ATTIC

The cat's in the attic

And she won't come down!

And every-time I'm near her,

She just runs round and round.

When suddenly a thought

Occurs to me!

There'll be little steps

Coming down the stairs

When she knows it's time for tea!

IF I WERE THE CAPTAIN OF A SPACESHIP FLIGHT

If I were the captain of a spaceship flight,

I wouldn't want to travel at the speed of light;

No, I'd like to orbit quite leisurely,

Gazing at the universe all in 3D,

Standing on the deck that's all high- tech,

Or sitting in the captain's chair,

I'd want to know what's out there:

The Plough, Orion, Pegasus (the Flying Horse),

And, of course, the Lion, the Bull and the Bear.

And if there is time in just one day,

I'd love to circle the Milky Way!

And if that means going through a meteor shower,

I'd want my ship to have special warp power,

And on my way back to one of the stars,

A quick 'beam down' and a potter on Mars,

Then back on the bridge, full speed ahead,

Safely home, how time has flown!

Time for tea, then off to bed.

A MAP IS LIKE SPAGHETTI

A map is like spaghetti that's been thrown on a plate.

If you forget to look at it, you may be very late!

So you must take time to see

Which roads go from A to B,

Like a spider's web of green and red,

Splashes of yellow too;

And then, of course, there's also the colour blue.

From city to city, the roads go on and on,

Wide and long,

With cars and lorries rushing by

As you sit and play a game of "I Spy".

So the next time there's spaghetti on a plate for you,

Try to make a map and build a road or two.

The smaller roads are B roads,

The medium roads are A,

And the largest of them all are called the motorways!

PLAYING A BOARD OR A CARD GAME

Shake, shake, shake! The luck is in your hands!

Throw out the dice or roll it and see where it lands.

Whether chance or guess or strategy,

People have played for centuries,

Rolling the dice of seeds or beads

Or playing the cards made out of reeds,

To match the suit or join the pairs

Or find the man with the frizzy hair;

So, once again, a shake of the hand!

If it's a seven, buy the Strand!

And did you know that in 1903

The Americans invented Monopoly?

Yes, games go back through history

Even as far as the years BC;

So instead of switching on your PC,

Sit around and play with your family!

RUGBY

Fifteen in a team

Like cogs in a machine

Crouching down,

Looking like a tortoise

Going round and round,

Under its legs

A ball like an egg!

Out it comes and then they run,

Pass, over the line,

A score of five!

The crowd comes alive

And then silence.

A kick over the crossbar,

Two points more to add to the score.

They play on with ten minutes to go.

The whistle blows!

It's seven, three

A great game of rugby!

STEAM TRAINS

Sometimes you may hear them hoot,

Billowing a trail of smoke and soot,

Running fast along the tracks.

Their faces black, the engine driver and his
mate

They can't be late!

" Put more coal on" as it chuff, chuff, chuffs its
way up the hills.

Heat like a furnace, boiling inside!

Turning the wheels Tic Tac Tic Tac

As the passengers ride

People sleep, babies cry

To take them north, south, east and west,

To work or rest.

Steam trains with names like Flying Scotsman,

Delivering parcels and post for the day

At every station along the way.

And now, though the coal has gone

To drive the engines on,

Replaced by diesel or electricity,

You can still see them or hear them whooping
away,

Reminding us all of yesterday!

THE RAINBOW

Where does it start?

And where does it end?

And how does it come

To be in the rain?

An archway to heaven,

Colours of seven;

Red and yellow,

Pink and green,

Purple and orange

And blue.

I can sing a rainbow

Can you?

CRICKET ON A WARM SUMMERS DAY

There's something very English

When cricket's being played

Upon the village green

On a warm summer's day.

The tick tock thwacks

When ball meets bat,

And if you miss it

You are out!

And they all shout "howzat!"

Each player in turn defending the wicket,

Hit, run, score, that's the game of cricket.

And as the light begins to fade,

Cream teas are put away,

The village settles down to rest,

Turns out its lights

And the hoot of the owl welcomes the night!

THE TAIL OF THE WAGGY DOG

Charlie's got a waggy tail

That spins round and round,

Not when he's asleep

Although sometimes when he's lying down.

Now, when I'm seeing so much energy,

I'm thinking 'electricity'!

Like the windmills on the hills ,

Which always need the wind;

But not the wag of Charlie's tail!

It's like his smile or a great big grin,

Made from happiness.

So I'll just look after him,

And always treat him right;

Then, maybe, one day

He might switch on the light!

THE CHRISTMAS ELVES

Though Christmas comes just once a year,

There's such a lot to prepare:

Sorting out the Christmas shelves

With all the other little elves,

And when that's done

We have so much fun

Filling up old Santa's sack

To fly around the world and back.

How does he do it with so much stuff?

He does it with fairy dust

And a magic puff!

CASTAWAY TOM AND THE RESCUE OF THE WHALE

Castaway Tom is very well known

For his adventures out at sea

And for the stories of his friends, the whales,

Who made a wave with their tails

To take him back home to Ducklesby.

With the gold he sold

He bought a small house,

And gave the rest to Charity.

One day, walking on a beach nearby,

Tom saw a stranded whale and heard it cry,

And soon a crowd gathered around

And pulled on a rope someone had found;

"One, two, three! Heave-ho! One, two, three! Heave- ho!"

They watched the whale go out to sea,

Dipping and diving with the whole family!

SWALLOWS FLYING HIGH

They can tell us the weather

They can tell us the time

Swallows flying high

The weather will be fine... Tomorrow

But flying low

"Oh no!"

There's rain to follow.

That's because they know

They fly where the midges go

Then later on

Night time calls

The hoot of the owls

As the shadows fall.

And in the morning, they sing

There's so much to learn

Because nature is a wonderful thing.

SUNSET

As the evening shadows fade

And make way for the creatures of the night,

The moon just gently smiles

As the sun turns out its light.